EMBARKING ON SURVIVAL

A MOVING ODYSSEY

MAMPAD PP RASHEED
TRANSLATED BY YASEEM FAYAD

Made with ♥ on the Notion Press Platform
www.notionpress.com

Contents

Contents

EMBARKING ON SURVIVAL

a moving odyssey

About the translator :

Mr. Yaseem Fayad, born in 2004 into an expatriate family of Riyadh, Saudi Arabia had completed his primary and high schooling over there. Now, he pursues his Arts Degree in English Literature from MES Mampad College, the only rural autonomous institution of Kerala, India. He has undertook and coordinated many social welfare programs for the downtrodden and differently abled during his tenure as the secretary of National Service Scheme of his college.

A Hundred Thousand Thanks

to all my family and friends
ALSO;
Kunjunni Mash, Renowned Malayalam Poet
Rahul Gandhi, Member of Parliament
A. P. Anilkumar, Member of Legislative Assembly, Kerala
Jafar Malik I. A. S., Former District Collector, Malappuram
Syed Munavvar Ali Shihab, IUML
Dr. K Sivankutty, Teacher and Writer
Basheer Mampuram, Differently Abled People's League
Manaf Medappil, Differently Abled People's League
Philip Mampad, ASI Malappuram District (for translation)
Dr. Manzur Ali, Principal, MES Mampad College (Foreword)
Dr. Sajid A Latheef, Assistant Professor, MES Mampad College
Jify Marjan, a gifted artist (image on the cover)
Aqib Javid & Avanthika O. (Cover Layout)
Mohammed Bassim, Friend and Well Wisher

AND ALL KIND HEARTED PEOPLE IN THIS JOURNEY

Foreword

"However difficult life may seem, there is always something you can do and succeed at."

-Stephen Hawking

In a world where each individual is distinct, it is the celebration of our diversity that truly enriches our lives. People with different abilities have often demonstrated to us the incredible power of the human spirit. It gives me great pleasure to introduce this book, Athijeevanathinte Aadyapaadam written by Mampad P P Rasheed in Malayalam which is translated into English by Mr Yaseem Fayad, BA English student. The book highlights the struggles, achievements, and distinctive viewpoints of the author on people with disabilities. The author writes in the book that perseverance and determined mind will turn problems into possibilities.

Insulting and ridiculing differently-abled people was pretty frequent even in my childhood, which could have been passed down through generations. People with physical and mental infirmities, according to Hitler, were "useless" to society and "unworthy of life". As you travel through the pages of this English translation, I advise you to have an open heart and mind to the incredible experiences that await you. Let these stories serve as a reminder that every person, regardless of talents or limitations, has an important role to play in our society.

Language has the power to bring people together, and it is through the written word that we can build bridges of understanding and empathy. This translation work, done with great passion and attention, allows us to share the stories and voices of individuals with disabilities with a wider audience. We hope that by making these true experiences available in English, we may foster more understanding and compassion in our community.

The translator Mr. Yaseem Fayad has done just to the original script in Malayalam. I'd like to cite a few phrases that will touch your heart. "*A caring heart knows no boundaries and may reside in the farthest reaches of the world, ready to lend a hand and offer help.*" "*Defects are woven into the very fabric of life. Yet, amidst these imperfections, a profound journey of self-discovery unfolds, particularly for the differently-abled who possess an unparalleled strength.*"

I want to express my profound gratitude to the translator, author, editor, and everyone else who helped make this project a reality. Finally, I'd like to remind everyone that true power rests in our ability to embrace variety, demonstrate empathy, and create a more inclusive world.

Manzur Ali P P, PhD
Principal, MES Mampad College(Autonomous)

Preface

I begin this third edition of my book with a profound sense of gratitude, extending my warm thanks to all the readers who embraced the previous editions wholeheartedly. Your support and encouragement have been the driving force behind my continued journey as an author. My inspiration to write this book came from observing differently abled individuals who, despite facing numerous challenges, often seemed content with complacency.

Through this book, I hope to convey a message that readers can interpret in their own way. In recent times, government and societal care for the differently abled have reached new heights. It is incumbent upon each member of our community to maximize the opportunities provided to us and actively participate in shaping a society where we take charge of our destinies with responsibility. I personally escaped the confinement of my room through relentless hard work and unwavering determination. Without this, I might have become someone perpetually reliant on sympathy and the helping hands of others. I owe my heartfelt thanks to numerous individuals who have been instrumental in the transformative journey I've undertaken.

First and foremost, my deepest gratitude goes to my mother and sisters, who have showered me with love and compassion since my birth. They never allowed my disability to isolate me within our home, even though our circumstances couldn't always support my writing aspirations. Our neighbors and society have also shown me immeasurable kindness. Special mention goes to those who facilitated my education at home, including Kunjunni Mash, Paul Valayil, Abdul Jabbar Mash, Sivankutty Mash, and later, Abdul Salam, Fayis K, Ashraf Tana, Firdous, Sunil, Ummer, and the benevolent Panakkad Sadiq Ali Shihab Thangal.

I apologize for not being able to mention everyone's name here, but your contributions are cherished. December 31, 2018, marked a significant milestone in my life when I became a government employee. I extend my gratitude to the Government of Kerala and all those involved for understanding my situation and offering me a job. A special mention goes to Badarussaman E, who gifted me an electronic wheelchair at a differently abled gathering in Parappanangadi. This gift transformed my life, granting me the ability to explore the world independently, like a bird with wings. I'd also like to express my gratitude to the educational institutions, teachers, students, and their guardians in my locality, as they are the readers of this book.

The officials of MES Mampad College, including OP Abdurrahman Sir, Dr. Nisthar Sir, Principal Manzur Ali, and others, deserve a standing ovation. I also acknowledge the support from NSS, NCC, YRC, Dr. Haseena Madam, former union chairman Nihal Wandoor, Shahala Malik, and fellow students. I would be remiss not to mention Muhammed Shaheen, whose tireless efforts for the differently abled community are commendable. Additionally, the opportunity to showcase the first edition of this book at the Sharjah International Book Fair in 2021, with the assistance of Dubai KMCC and my friend Haris Babu Mampad, was a memorable experience.

In conclusion, I extend my heartfelt gratitude to Mr. Yaseem Fayad for his invaluable contribution to the publication of this third edition. His dedication and exceptional translation skills have brought this book to life, and his commitment to the welfare of the differently abled is truly remarkable. This book represents a small collection of my experiences and knowledge, and it is my fervent hope that it may inspire and energize differently abled individuals and those who care for them.

THANK YOU!

CHAPTER ONE

First Step in Survival

I have never seen people lacking enthusiasm when welcoming and celebrating the beginning of a year. Singing and dancing mark the start of this momentous occasion. Many of us view this specific time as an opportunity to bring about change, break free from addictions, or end any harmful habits. However, in my humble opinion, waiting until the start of a year is not necessary to ignite a spark of change in our lives. Whether it's a year, a month, a week, a day, an hour, or even a second, every unit of time has the potential to trigger a significant transformation in the course of our lives.

From the very first heartbeat in our mother's womb to the last one on our deathbed, each of us continually strives to survive and adapt. Time bring about constant changes, sometimes occurring in a fraction of a second. Nothing in this vast universe remains stationary; everything moves through its orbits. Therefore, why should we underestimate our potential and wait for a specific time like the start of a year to make a change?

Time itself is one of the greatest opportunities we possess, yet people often fail to recognize its true value. I believe that we must live each moment of our lives under the rays of hope, with full enthusiasm, and by understanding the various chapters of survival. Regardless of the obstacles we face, we must be brave enough to swim against the current, much like the fish that defend against the strong currents until they reach the shore of self-satisfaction and contentment. Victory belongs to those who energetically move forward until they achieve their goals.

For this reason, I have named this book 'First Step in Survival,' as I have come to realize that many individuals, both abled and differently-abled, find themselves dwelling in the darkness of negative thoughts and self-doubt. It is my belief that we should embrace each moment with optimism and strive to live life to its fullest potential. With determination and courage, we can overcome challenges and find fulfillment in our journey.

CHAPTER TWO

HANDICAPPED? WHO?

When we hear the question "Who are handicapped?", an image of a physically or mentally challenged individual often comes to mind. However, upon deeper reflection, we realize that this perspective is somewhat shallow, and certain insights come to light.

After much contemplation and research, I have arrived at a simple conclusion: a task performed by an able person may not be replicated by a disabled person in the same amount of time, but they can still complete it, either partially or fully, if given ample time. Let's consider an example; a mentally and physically able librarian effortlessly lends books to readers and records it in a register. On the other hand, a disabled librarian may do the same task, but at a slower pace, taking their limitations into account. In essence, both parties accomplish the job; the only difference lies in the time taken for doing it.

"Disabled are those who think of themselves that they cannot do anything!" This realization answers my dilemma of who really is differently abled. If a physically healthy person believes that they are incapable of doing anything, are they handicapped? No, they might be facing serious mental challenges. On the other hand, a differently abled person must possess sheer determination and courage to overcome hurdles and find their space to thrive.

In the past, society had a reluctant mindset towards differently abled individuals, but thankfully now, educational developments and social changes have led to a more inclusive scenario. Journalists have played a vital role in shedding light on the conditions of differently abled people, and various organizations are tirelessly working for their rights. Hereby, I would like to establish the fact that there are many differently-abled individuals who perceive themselves as a 'good for nothing'. This perspective needs to be changed, and they should be encouraged to march competitively towards victory. With determination, support, and a shift in societal attitudes, differently-abled individuals can achieve great things and they also can lead fulfilling lives.

CHAPTER THREE

A Rewind

When we reflect on our experiences, we come face to face with profound truths. This becomes evident when we consider how differently-abled individuals perceive the world and how society views them.

Not too long ago, a physically challenged newborn was often seen as a curse or rather a symbol of divine anger. Regardless of gender, such infants were treated as tragic figures, isolated even within their own families. Shockingly, parents played a pivotal role in perpetuating this attitude, driven by reasons ranging from the belief that raising a seemingly useless creature was futile to thoughts of ending its life. Consequently, many of these individuals lived a life of suffering, feeling like a burden or a curse, enduring both birth and death.

As someone who has worked for the welfare of differently-abled individuals for over 20 years, I am well aware of the stereotypes they face. Some people wrongly believe that having a challenged family member brings disgrace to the family, decreases acceptance from relatives and society, and brings difficulties and hardships in raising the child. There is even fear of genetic disabilities being passed on to future generations. These unfounded fears lead some households to hide their differently-abled members during special occasions, striving to maintain a facade of flawlessness.

Yet, amidst all the celebration next door, few realize the anguish of a solitary individual confined to the shadows. Disabilities are not always a result of inherent problems; accidents or momentary carelessness can also lead to physical handicaps. Accepting fate and finding the energy to rise and move forward is essential in such situations.

If a family can embrace a child with disabilities without fear, recognizing the child's individuality and affording them the same rights and liberties as any other child, magic can happen, even if the disability is profound. While an able-bodied baby may require only ordinary parenting, a child with disabilities calls for extraordinary care and support. Unfortunately, it's not uncommon to see disabled children being segregated from so-called "abled" ones, treated unequally, and denied the same amenities and attention.

This is not only foolish but also unjustifiable. It infringes upon their fundamental rights and perpetuates delusions that only able-bodied individuals can achieve greatness while the disabled are destined to remain in darkness forever. Such attitudes need to change for the betterment of our differently-abled friends.

We have inspiring examples throughout history, like Helen Keller, Beethoven, and Stephen Hawking, who were all differently-abled and contributed significantly to making the world a better place. Remember the childhood story of Edison, who was labeled as mentally ill but went on to become one of the greatest inventors in history, thanks to his mother's determination to educate him at home.

Parents should never worry about their disabled children but instead empower them to thrive alongside their peers. One particular family comes to my mind—a couple blessed with a child after a long wait. Initially, the child appeared perfect, but as time passed, developmental delays became apparent. Despite this, the parents decided to dedicate their lives to the betterment of their child, even sacrificing high-paying jobs. They made a brave choice to focus solely on their child's well-being and education, relocating to Switzerland for better opportunities.

Eventually, the child passed the matriculation examination, and their family's smiling picture holds a special place in my heart. This story shows us the strength of love and dedication that can transform lives. Let us remember that differently-abled individuals deserve equal opportunities and support, just like any other member of society. By fostering inclusivity and understanding, we can create a world where everyone can shine.

CHAPTER FOUR

Empowering the Differently Abled: Breaking Barriers, Unlocking Opportunities

Regardless of the financial backgrounds of the families they are born into, the differently abled often find themselves facing hardships and loneliness. However, their determination and support from family can lead them to rise above their challenges and fulfill their dreams. Unfortunately, in families struggling with financial difficulties, the lack of proper care and company may confine the differently abled within the four walls of a room, hindering their ability to learn and grow. It is crucial for parents to understand that providing proper care to differently abled children is paramount, and this responsibility remains the same regardless of a family's wealth. Some affluent families may resort to paying substantial fees to special schools or day care institutions to distance themselves from the perceived "disturbance."

In these situations, the differently abled individuals lose the invaluable companionship of their parents. To put this into perspective, imagine the difficulties faced during a temporary physical fracture, and then consider the lifetime dependence and isolation experienced by differently abled individuals. Furthermore, females among the differently abled face an even more challenging situation, as they have additional needs that require support from others. Their struggles often go unheard, confined within the four walls of their homes, yet they manage to navigate through life with remarkable ease.

Back in times, differently abled children were often admitted to schools close to their homes, but as they progressed to upper primary levels, their education was suspended due to the lack of suitable institutions nearby. This abrupt end to their educational journey deprives them of opportunities for personal growth and development, leaving them feeling trapped like birds in a cage.

We must strive for a society that uproots the obstacles in their path and paves the way for their success. Every individual deserves the opportunity to study, excel, and secure gainful employment, showcasing their skills and talents in mechanical, technical, artistic, and hospitality fields. In order to achieve this, it is essential to ensure convenient access for wheelchairs and scooters to the residences of differently abled individuals. Worship centers must also have facilities that accommodate their mobility needs, allowing them to participate in prayers.

Encouraging entrepreneurship, the provision of interest-free loans and subsidies for business ventures can empower the differently abled to become self-reliant. Additionally, creating opportunities for government employment and cottage industries will open avenues for them to contribute to society. Further tax exemptions on home, electricity, and water bills will alleviate their financial burdens. Offering computer handling training and laptops or desktops will equip eligible individuals for the job market. Companies should be encouraged to employ the differently abled in 1:3 proportions for workplaces with five or more employees.

Government assistance should be extended to the dependents of completely bedridden disabled individuals. Ramps and enhanced accessible infrastructure at public and residential spaces will ensure inclusivity across all functions and events. Furthermore, reserving a proportion of lottery agencies for the differently abled can contribute to their financial well-being. Educating parents through awareness classes will enhance their understanding and ability to provide the best care for their differently abled children. Additionally, establishing enjoyable recreation centers at Gram Panchayats can foster a sense of community well being and spread joy among the differently abled.

Recognizing the financial challenges they may face, classifying all families with a differently abled member as B.P.L. (Below Poverty Line) will ensure they receive the necessary support. Furthermore, issuing licenses for selling handicrafts at regular intervals across the state will promote self-employment opportunities.

Scholarships for the differently abled should be reviewed and increased to encourage and assist them in pursuing education. Finally, early teaching of sign language and Braille will promote inclusive education from a young age. By implementing these initiatives, we can build a society that empowers the differently abled, breaking the barriers for them and unlocking their true potential.

CHAPTER FIVE

EMBRACING IMPERFECTIONS: THE UNYIELDING SPIRIT OF THE DIFFERENTLY ABLED

In the vast expanse of our world, imperfections intertwine with existence, giving rise to an unyielding truth: nothing under the sky is without its flaws. From the mightiest forces of nature to the tiniest atom, defects are woven into the very fabric of life. Yet, amidst these imperfections, a profound journey of self-discovery unfolds, particularly for the differently-abled who possess an unparalleled strength.

In this tapestry of life, all creatures, great and small, bear disabilities. From the crashing waves of untimely rains to the upheaval of tsunamis, nature too displays its flaws. Within families, the dance of arguments and conflicts unveils yet another facet of defects. Societal ailments, bred by superstitions and malevolent customs, add to the list of imperfections. Even in the realm of politics, where selfless service often succumbs to self-interest, we witness imperfections.

Bearing all these defects, the courage and tenacity displayed by the differently abled is surprisingly unmatched. It is a testament to the power of unwavering faith in an invisible force that many believe in and seek solace from. Why, then, should these individuals, who find comfort in the intangible, not stride forward with the legs they lack? Their seemingly frail hands possess the strength to seize victory at great heights. How can one be blind when their hearts emit words so courageous and inspiring?

To fathom the divine majesty hidden in the void, we must first become aware of our own capabilities. Armed with self-awareness, we craft plans to challenge our limitations, to rise above adversity. Let us not falter but strive with unyielding determination, for it is through this fierce resolve that we usher forth transformative change in society. History reminds us that greatness is not borne of shortcuts, but by possessing a resilient spirit and a resolute mind. Too often, blame for misfortune is placed upon circumstances and the past. Yet, as true luminaries have shown, greatness is forged in the crucible of challenges. The differently abled must perceive these tough times as opportunities for growth, a chance to rise from the ashes, and embrace their inner fortitude.

Regrettably, the talents of the differently abled often go unnoticed and disregarded, even within their own homes. However, this should not deter them, for like mischievous plays, their brilliance awaits an audience. The world may not yet recognize their worth, but within these souls lie the power to amaze and inspire. Seeking wisdom from experienced souls and relentlessly pursuing one's passions opens the gates to a world of boundless possibilities. In the age of interconnectedness, digital platforms serve as canvases to showcase our talents, allowing our brilliance to illuminate the world.

In the face of indifference, remember that true neighbors transcend mere proximity. A caring heart knows no boundaries and may reside in the farthest reaches of the world, ready to lend a hand and offer help.

In this magnificent tapestry of life, imperfections are threads that enrich the fabric of existence. The resolute spirit of the differently abled proves that limitations need not shackle our potential. With determination, self-awareness, and the unwavering support of true neighbors, we embark on a journey of discovery, where the brilliance of each soul illuminates the universe. Together, let us celebrate imperfections and embrace triumphs, fostering a world that cherishes the untold strength within us all.

CHAPTER SIX

The Gift of Differently Abled Children: A Journey of Blessings

As parents of differently abled children, we should not feel sorry for ourselves. For believers, this could be understood in a more convenient way. Their belief in a higher power teaches us that He is the Exalted, the Most Merciful, and the Just. We must understand that being chosen to care for a special child is a divine blessing. Only a select few couples are entrusted with such precious souls, and there is a deeper purpose behind this selection.

Imagine the most precious thing you possess, something you cherish and protect with utmost care. You wouldn't entrust it to just anyone, but after much consideration, you would choose a patient, trustworthy, and truthful person from your circle to safeguard it.

This analogy beautifully reflects the role of parents of differently abled children. God, in His wisdom, has chosen us to care for these unique souls, knowing that we possess the qualities necessary for this sacred responsibility.

This journey is a test of our faith, resilience, and love. Your selection as a parent of a differently abled child is a testament to your strength and virtue. Through this experience, you earn heavenly rewards within a short span of time. You gain profound insights into the realities of life, enabling you to live with a higher purpose and act differently. Your path becomes distinct, taking you on a journey that only a few have embraced. Unknowingly, you become competitors, not in the conventional sense, but in the spiritual realm.

Indeed, life is a competition, a test of character, and endurance. It challenges us with poverty and prosperity, pushing us to strive and adapt. Every living being competes with nature from birth, vying to survive and thrive. As humans, we too compete, but not against each other. Our real competition is to navigate life's challenges, to become the best version of ourselves, and to fulfill our unique purpose.

Differently abled individuals are no less eligible as competitors, but society sometimes sidelines them due to various reasons. We must remember that the struggles and triumphs of human life were designed to encourage survival of the fittest. However, this doesn't mean that laughter should only belong to the privileged while the less fortunate cry. Both scenes are avoided if worked accordingly. Let us come together as a compassionate and inclusive society. Instead of pity or sympathy, let us offer support, understanding, and opportunities to differently abled individuals and their families. Their unique perspectives and experiences enrich our world and inspire us to embrace life's challenges with grace and gratitude.

Dear parents, cherish the divine gift you have received. Embrace your role with love and devotion, for your journey is one of blessings and enlightenment. Your child may be differently abled, but the love they bring into your life is boundless, teaching you profound lessons of compassion, resilience, and the true essence of humanity. Embrace this journey wholeheartedly, for it is an extraordinary path that leads to an extraordinary life.

CHAPTER SEVEN

Life with Differently Abled Individuals: A Journey of Hope

Life takes a unique turn for those who decide to share their journey with differently abled partners. Whether it's the husband or the wife, they undertake a noble task, sacrificing their own dreams to navigate the challenges that life presents. The bond formed between two pure hearts is not defined by money, glory, or material comforts but by the deep empathy they share.

Before entering into such partnerships, it is crucial for the families of both the bride and groom to be transparent and understanding. Pressurizing anyone into such a commitment can lead to unhappiness and strain in the relationship. True love and contentment can only flourish when both partners genuinely embrace and cherish each other. It is also vital to recognize that differently abled individuals do not seek sympathy but an empathetic support system from their circle of family and friends. Offering assistance and encouragement without waiting for them to ask for help can nurture a blooming garden of love. Understanding their needs and valuing their time can build a stronger bond of trust and mutual respect.

Dear differently challenged readers,

We all depend on others for our needs, but we also strive to fulfill them independently whenever possible. By putting in efforts to compliment our caregivers and family, we can overcome laziness and embrace self-reliance. Recognizing the value of small achievements will empower us to face life's challenges with confidence and contentment, proving that we are not burdens but contributors to our families. Change is an undeniable truth of life. Embracing change allows us to conquer tough challenges and grow as individuals. We should be open to change, welcoming it as an opportunity for progress and improvement. As the universe evolves every second, so do us, and we must harness this power of change to shape our destiny.

To those who doubt their abilities, let us dispel negativity and kindle hope. Each of us has the potential to live a meaningful life, regardless of how we were born. Our worth lies in how we lived, not in the circumstances of our birth. Knowledge and education are vital tools to navigate life's journey and soar to new heights. We, too, possess the fundamental rights of any individual and should claim our rightful place in society. Instead of dwelling on limitations, let us seek inspiration from those who have turned their disabilities into strengths. Let us recognize that we are an integral part of society and can make meaningful contributions. Life's brevity reminds us to live fully and embrace knowledge and wisdom to shine brightly.

So, dear readers, let us embrace life with courage, resilience, and optimism. We may have faced challenges, but we must remember that wisdom is the light that dispels darkness. Let us rise above any obstacles and celebrate the beauty of life, one that knows no boundaries and is enriched by our unique journeys. Remember, it is the journey that defines us, not the starting point.

CHAPTER EIGHT

Fostering Inclusivity for the Differently Abled: A Shared Responsibility

Addressing the challenges faced by the differently abled requires a collaborative effort between the government and society. One crucial step is to establish special seating areas for them at government offices and ensure that their concerns are promptly addressed. This can be achieved by appointing special officers or assigning the task to existing officers. Additionally, offices situated on upper floors should provide accessible counters so that differently abled individuals can easily handle their requests without facing unnecessary difficulties and time wastage. When constructing footpaths, it is essential to consider the needs of the differently abled. By building ramps on both ends of the footpaths, we can create a more inclusive environment where pedestrians and those using wheelchairs or scooters can travel together seamlessly.

The right to worship is a fundamental human right, yet many worship places lack proper facilities for differently abled individuals. Mosques, churches, and temples should be constructed with ramps to ensure that everyone, regardless of their physical abilities, can offer prayers at their holy places. It is our responsibility to provide equal access and consideration to the differently abled when designing and constructing these places of worship. Recreation centers and tourist destinations should also be made accessible for the differently abled. For instance, at the Conolly's Plot in Nilambur, where the World's largest planted Teak is located, constructing a ramp on the massive steps after the hanging bridge would allow everyone to experience its magnificence.

Organizations working for the welfare of differently abled individuals should strive to advocate for their rights and ensure that their demands are brought before the government in various developmental projects. By making the government aware of the challenges they face, we can work towards a more inclusive society.

On special occasions and celebrations throughout the year, such as Republic Day, Independence Day, and during religious festivals, efforts should be made to include the differently abled in the festivities. Allowing them to participate actively, like carrying a tricolor flag or being part of cultural events, will promote societal equality and strengthen our democracy.

Fostering inclusivity for the differently abled is a shared responsibility. By working together, the government, society, and various organizations can create a more accessible and accommodating environment for all individuals, regardless of their abilities. Let us strive to build a society where the rights and needs of the differently abled are fully recognized and respected, making our nation truly inclusive and diverse.

CHAPTER NINE

Empowering the Differently Abled through Education and Inclusivity

Kerala prides itself on being a state with complete literacy, but as someone working for the rights of the differently abled, I have witnessed the challenges they face in accessing proper education. Though the situation has improved, there is still much to be done to ensure that they receive the education they rightfully deserve. It is heart-wrenching to see children of the same age heading to school with colorful bags and umbrellas, while some among them are denied this basic right due to their disabilities. However, we must not accept failure in such situations; instead, we must view disability as a call for resurrection. Every differently abled individual should have access to education as it is essential for building a healthy society. Education enriches one's knowledge, and a culturally aware citizen can bring about positive changes in society. Education knows no boundaries and is a fundamental right that should be guaranteed by the government and society.

For those above 18 years of age who missed out on formal education, the state government is offering equivalent classes and exams for various grade levels through the Kerala State Literacy Mission. Extending this scheme further into the realm of the differently abled could prove beneficial. However, we must also address the challenges they face in accessing these centers. Convenient and accessible locations should be arranged to ensure they do not face unnecessary hardships.

Many differently abled individuals gather weekly at Palliative Care Centers or Day Care centers within their Panchayats, where they enjoy a leisurely day filled with singing, dancing, and laughter, providing a brief respite from their daily struggles. Creating a learning environment in these centers would be immensely helpful, fostering a calm and serene atmosphere conducive to their development. Adequate staffing at these centers would also contribute to the overall progress of the differently abled.

Based on their physical and mental well-being, computer literacy can also be provided to them, opening opportunities in fields like Photoshop, Graphic Designing, and Online Marketing, where they can excel. As part of a drive to make them independent, it is encouraging to witness a shift in society's perception towards differently abled individuals.

The journey towards inclusive education for the differently abled continues, and we must strive to make education accessible to all. By providing learning opportunities and fostering a supportive environment, we can empower them to achieve their full potential and become valuable contributors to society. Let us work together to break down barriers and create a world where everyone, regardless of their abilities, is embraced and celebrated.

CHAPTER TEN

Face Foundation of India: A Beacon of Hope and Inclusion

Among charitable organizations, Face Foundation stands out for its unique approach towards humanitarian activities. Headquartered in Malappuram, the organization's vision to uplift mentally, physically, and economically challenged individuals is truly commendable. It seeks to integrate the marginalized into mainstream society by offering opportunities for their mental and physical development. At Face Foundation, differently abled individuals are not just recipients of help; they are empowered to lend a helping hand and contribute meaningfully to society.

Numerous patrons have played a pivotal role in supporting this esteemed organization, and while I may not recall all their names, I extend my gratitude and prayers for their well-being and success. Janab Naheem Saheb, PK Anwar Naha, Janab Naseer Melethil, Janab Naseer, Samad Master, and Dr. Yasir, along with countless others, have been instrumental in the Foundation's noble mission. My encounter with Face Foundation came in 2016 when a friend mentioned their unique approach during a program at the Palliative center. Intrigued by their philosophy, I eagerly pledged to participate in their upcoming camp for differently abled individuals named 'INSPIRE-3' on 24th December. However, it remained just a wish until fate intervened. I stumbled upon an advertisement for the camp, and with excitement and curiosity, my wife Safiya and I prepared to close our shop and embark on this transformative journey.

Having never changed my sleeping location except for medical treatments, the prospect of the camp brought both anticipation and anxiety. As we neared Parappanangadi, the warmth and hospitality of the gas station workers reassured us. Soon, we witnessed a vibrant village bustling with happiness and heard cheerful announcements over microphones. Differently abled people from across the state alighted from various vehicles, and the long queue of volunteers at the Palathingal School Compound reaffirmed their dedication to this noble cause.

Upon parking, we were embraced by a group of helpful volunteers. They attended to every detail, taking me out of the car, caring for our luggage, and offering a wheelchair for my convenience. It was a sight that left my family and me astonished. In this compassionate environment, there was no room for marginalization or avoidance. Instead, everyone had a role to play, united in their commitment to create an inclusive and supportive atmosphere.

My worries faded away in the presence of these caring souls. Dr. Yasir, Samad Master, and Naseer Master came to meet me, and a cameraman captured our interaction. They were delighted to learn about the writer and motivator within me. As I presented them with copies of my book, they expressed the urgent need for more individuals like me in society.

Face Foundation of India sets an exemplary standard for societies and organizations. Their compassionate approach to empowering the differently abled is an inspiration to us all. Through their efforts, countless lives are transformed, and the barriers that once held back the marginalized are shattered. Let us join hands with such organizations, fostering a world where every individual, regardless of their abilities, is embraced with love, care, and respect. Together, we can create a more inclusive and harmonious society for all.

CHAPTER ELEVEN

Empowering the Differently Abled: A Testament of Hope

The garden organized by Face Foundation bloomed with hope and inspiration as individuals celebrated their freedom. The volunteers, with their innate virtue, played the role of angels, igniting dreams and fostering progress, overcoming obstacles with their unwavering support. This gathering provided a platform for differently abled individuals to share ideas, dreams, and realize their place in society. Many who were previously dependent on their families discovered newfound independence through reading, writing, and excelling in higher-level examinations. Skill development classes in areas such as tailoring, computer knowledge, and graphic designing opened doors to brighter futures.

The purpose of such camps, like Face Foundation, is to help individuals develop their personalities, motivation, and job-related skills. The organization's care and compassion left a lasting impact, prompting even those who were hesitant to leave home to embrace the experience for at least one week. During the camp, various programs like employment training and personality development classes were conducted, and skill development workshops led by eminent personalities revitalized our solitary lives. As a participant, I decided to learn graphic designing and joined the course with eager determination. The environment provided a supportive setting, with classrooms thoughtfully designed to accommodate everyone's needs, including ramps for wheelchair accessibility. The volunteers went above and beyond to ensure each individual felt valued and cared for.

Daily routines were organized with care and attention. Early mornings began with a hot cup of tea, administered with kindness and consideration for those who needed assistance. After attending to primary needs, prayers were offered according to one's religion, and motivation classes were conducted by various religious leaders. The camp encouraged a sense of community and inclusivity, where individuals freely interacted and learned from one another. Cultural programs in the evenings were a vibrant celebration of talent nurtured by the organization, leaving unforgettable memories. Each day concluded with personalized dinner, and guests visited each other's rooms, fostering camaraderie and friendship.

I recall my first experience attending Jumua prayer, a rare opportunity granted by Face Foundation. Tears welled up in the eyes of fellow attendees as they witnessed my joy and surprise. The mosque's ground floor, accessible by ramps, warmly welcomed differently abled individuals. The inspiring sight of a completely blind individual leading the prayer demonstrated that intellectual ability is paramount, surpassing physical limitations. As the differently abled, we should see our disabilities as opportunities to discover our talents, polish them, and become valuable contributors to society. Our skills define us more than our disabilities ever will. Instead of focusing on the percentage of our disabilities, let us emphasize the percentage of our skills and use them to triumph over challenges. It is essential for society to recognize that the differently abled are not burdens but powerful contributors. We are an integral part of the economy, and our potential to thrive, when nurtured, can uplift the entire community.

Let us celebrate our abilities, support one another, and work towards a society where all individuals, regardless of their abilities, are valued, respected, and empowered to reach their fullest potential. The differently abled have much to offer, and with collective efforts, we can create a more inclusive and compassionate world.

CHAPTER TWELVE

Parents: The Pillars of Love and Support

Our parents are the foundation of our existence on this beautiful earth, and it is our responsibility as differently abled individuals to hold them close, nurture them, and make their lives colorful with love and care. Despite our physical limitations, we should never shy away from fulfilling our duties towards our parents, as their happiness is the true essence of our lives.

Just as we provide chocolates and ice creams to our children, we must also ensure that our parents have everything they need. It is essential to show them that we are fully capable of looking after them just like anyone else. Life's game can be won with love and devotion to our parents, and the joy they experience from our efforts will be just as delightful as the happiness our children feel when they taste the fruits of our hard work. For differently abled individuals, making pilgrimages to places like Mecca, Medina, Sabarimala, or Malayattoor may be less feasible. However, we need not feel deprived of a serene spiritual experience. Instead, we can take pride in caring for our parents and creating a bond that surpasses any pilgrimage.

A story of Pakkanar reminds us that divine blessings can be attained through acts of kindness and charity towards the poor, needy, and elderly. We need not seek divine blessings solely through elaborate trips; rather, we can find spirituality in caring for those around us, especially our parents, who have selflessly sacrificed their lives for our well-being.

Sadly, in today's world, we witness a concerning trend where some individuals leave their parents behind to manage their homes like mere caretakers while they embark on lavish trips. It is crucial to remember that parents have devoted their entire lives to their children, sacrificing their own dreams and desires to ensure our happiness and success. It is disheartening to see them left behind while their children indulge in self-centered pursuits. As differently abled individuals, we should strive to set an example by showering our parents with love, respect, and care. They deserve our utmost attention, especially in their golden years when they should be enjoying life's pleasures, not feeling neglected and abandoned.

Let us cherish our parents and celebrate their presence in our lives. By being there for them with genuine affection and compassion, we can create a meaningful and fulfilling journey together, enriching each other's lives with love and support. Remember, what we give to our parents will be mirrored in the love and care we receive from our own children in the future.

CHAPTER THIRTEEN

Rahana - A Melody of Resilience

Rahana, a dear friend from my locality, was a graduate, an avid reader, and a gifted singer. Despite her ongoing battle with illness, she would occasionally visit my cosmetic shop on her way to Snehatheeram Palliative Centre in Chungathara, where she found solace and camaraderie among nearly a hundred others from Nilambur Taluk. At Snehatheeram, they experienced a vibrant festival of joy and laughter, providing them with care, love, and inspiration. Rahana's indomitable spirit kept her going, despite her struggles with diabetes and the need for regular dialysis.

As life took us on separate paths, we communicated through phone calls, and Rahana always shared her challenges and realizations with me. Her hardships were numerous, perhaps more than anyone should endure in a lifetime. The physical distance and her deteriorating health made it challenging for us to meet as frequently. One night, she called me, expressing her sorrow over our decreased interactions. She spoke of my writing and how my tales of survival inspired her, even though I faced an 85% physical disability. Amidst her distress, she confided in me about her doctor's advice to amputate her big toe to prevent further complications. Initially hesitant, she later chose to proceed with the surgery after our conversation. I encouraged her to consider the bigger picture, reminding her of the other fingers and toes she still possessed. Rather than dwelling on what she lacked, I urged her to appreciate what she had. It was like removing negativity from her heart, I told her, and tried my best to motivate her as a supportive brother.

After weeks of silence, she called me with unexpected news. She had changed her mind and, with her family's support, underwent the surgery to remove her big toe. The doctor was curious about the sudden shift, and Rahana credited me as the source of her newfound courage. I was touched and congratulated her warmly. I encouraged her to face life with unwavering courage, assuring her that a compassionate listener can alleviate the burden of the speaker.

Rahana's caring nature converted to her concern for other physically challenged individuals. She raised the issue of a malfunctioning wall fan in the dialysis center of Nilambur Taluk Hospital. Me being a part of the All Kerala Wheelchair Rights Federation, Nilambur Chapter, took immediate action, and within a week, her request was fulfilled, and the wall fan was installed. The fan continues to bring comfort to patients in loving memory of Rahana.

On that fateful day, August 10, 2018, Rahana's life journey came to an end. She endured hardships from the tender age of nine, leaving behind a legacy of unmatched pain and resilience. May her soul rest in peace in the embrace of a heavenly abode. Heartfelt condolences to a remarkable soul who touched our hearts with her strength and courage.

CHAPTER FOURTEEN

A Tale of Unyielding Love: Kareem and Asmatha

Dear readers, when we think of differently-abled individuals who inspire us, names like Helen Keller, Stephen Hawking, and Nick often come to mind. Yet, there are unsung heroes among us who live their lives with limited abilities, facing countless challenges but still serving as a source of inspiration.

In my endeavor to write a book that embraces the stories of such individuals, I realized the importance of highlighting families like Kareem and Asmatha's. While society has seen instances where females hesitate to marry physically disabled men, or husbands abandon their wives after accidents or illnesses, there are exceptional souls who defy these norms. Kareem stands as a testament for this uncommon love and dedication.

Born into a poverty-stricken family, Kareem's early years were fraught with hardship after the untimely loss of his parents. Raised in an orphanage, his dreams of independence, love, and family remained steadfast. Despite limited means, he found solace in football and an affectionate bond grew with Asmatha, the daughter of Thayyil Muhammad and Fatimah. Their love triumphed over societal resistance, and Kareem married Asmatha, savoring a life of happiness and contentment. Blessed with a daughter, their lives were seemingly perfect until a tragic accident altered their course. Asmatha's fall from a Muringa tree left her disabled below the waist, and the challenges of hospitals and medicines became a new reality.

Amidst adversity, Kareem's love for his wife flourished, becoming a beacon of strength for Asmatha. His unwavering support and care breathed a new life into her smile, and they faced each hurdle as one mind in two bodies. Financial struggles were abundant, but they refused to beg or compromise their dignity, relying solely on the goodness of willing hearts. Asmatha's indomitable spirit shines through, and her smile remains a radiant full moon in the darkest night. She embraces her disability, finding peace in the belief of a better future. Together, they weathered storms, and their love blossomed further with the arrival of another daughter. Though Asmatha battles health issues, her artistry, showcased in performances like the Oppana, captivates all who witness it. Their modest home, a tiled roof structure, holds tales of resilience and perseverance.

Kareem, a former expatriate, contemplates the idea of overseas work to alleviate their debts, but the thought of leaving Asmatha behind fills him with trepidation.

Instead, he dedicates himself to driving an auto-rickshaw, carefully coordinating his schedule to care for his family. Asmatha dreams of clearing their debts and renovating their home, yearning for a life of happiness. Kareem, on the other hand, grapples with the desire to work abroad while remaining steadfast in his commitment to his family.

Let us extend a big salute to both Kareem and Asmatha - symbols of love that transcends limitations. Their journey exemplifies the profound bond of husband and wife, and their resilience inspires us all to embrace life's challenges with grace and determination.

CHAPTER FIFTEEN

Embracing Differences: Sakeer Hussain's Heartwarming Generosity

In a world where privileged individuals often extend help to the marginalized, including the differently-abled, it is unfortunately common for such assistance to be overshadowed by the perception of their limitations. However, Sakeer Hussain stands apart from this norm. Let me share my personal encounter with this remarkable individual.

In the year 2016-17, my life was a mix of joy and sorrow. Thanks to the support of my family and friends, I moved into a new home, but this also meant leaving behind my old shop near Mampad Town. The following eight months were a challenging period, especially for my livelihood.

One day, as I sat pondering on the verandah of my new home, a white car stopped nearby, and a pleasant-looking young man approached me with a smile. He recognized me and my home, Baithurahma, and we engaged in a heartfelt conversation for about ten minutes. Learning that I was a writer and involved in differently-abled welfare organizations, he expressed his happiness. Discovering his passion for reading, I gifted him my books, "The Orphan and the Magic Bird" and "Marivillu."

Sakeer Hussain is a busy businessman, but that doesn't stop him from helping those in need quietly and without fanfare. He promised to visit me regularly and shared his contact details with a warm smile. Despite my protests, he discreetly slipped a 2000 rupees note into my pocket, assuring me it wasn't because of my disability but a token of appreciation for the accomplishments I achieved despite my limitations. His words resonated deeply within me. This encounter prompted profound reflections on how society perceives the marginalized. I admired Sakeer Hussain for being different from those who offer charity solely based on perceived shortcomings. Unfortunately, when it comes to the differently-abled, they often get portrayed through a lens of pity.

Sakeer Hussain Kizhisseri, however, is a compassionate wanderer who challenges this mindset. I still maintain a strong bond with this extraordinary individual and extend my warm greetings to him and his family. His big-hearted approach to helping others is truly inspiring, and I hope his example encourages more people to embrace and celebrate our differences.

CHAPTER SIXTEEN

TRAVELLING TO THE HAZE LAND

Ten compassionate individuals, including Muneer Ponmala, Rahman Elamkulam, and Imtiyaz Malappuram, embarked on a remarkable journey as volunteers of the Cherthunirtham Charitable Organization. This organization plays a vital role in supporting and empowering the differently-abled, helping them lead self-reliant lives. Through various initiatives, they provide livelihood opportunities, clear debts, and even enable physically challenged individuals to undertake the sacred Muslim pilgrimage, Umrah.

One such unforgettable event was a trip organized for 35 differently-abled individuals, including myself and my family. The journey began on February 14, 2020, from Malappuram. Boarding the tourist bus for the first time, I was accompanied by familiar faces, making the journey even more joyous. Thanks to the attentive care of the volunteers, the journey was smooth and seamless, defying the challenges typically associated with a trip for differently-abled individuals. During a Friday stop at a Mosque, arrangements were made for those who wished to access it, while others were comfortably seated in the Mosque's canteen area. The warmth and hospitality shown by Saifu Alanallur, Raihanath Mankada, Lailatha Jubilee, Jabir Pookottur, Favas Ponmala, Vishnu Malappuram, and Hashir Ponmala made the experience truly heartwarming.

Throughout the journey, we were treated to breathtaking views and laughter-filled moments, thanks to the humor of Kadeeja Kotakkal, Faisal Olippuzha, and Sabad. The serene atmosphere of Vagamon welcomed us in the evening, and despite the chilly winds, the almighty's mercy kept us safe. Our stay in Vagamon allowed us to appreciate the beauty of nature, gazing at the stars and sharing stories with the moon. The friendly and accessible rooms ensured that all differently-abled individuals, including my family, faced no hardships during our stay.

The next day, we ventured to a nearby hill with imposing rocks, nestled amidst picturesque tea gardens. The sight of parachutes and the beautiful grape gardens of Theni in Tamil Nadu left us mesmerized. We explored the grapevines in wheelchairs, enjoying ice creams and sarbat, creating a joyous and positive ambiance.

Completing the two-day trip under the banner of Cherthunirtham club left me humbled, realizing how vast and unimaginable the world truly is. I extend my heartfelt gratitude to all those behind this initiative and similar projects. Thank you all for making this journey so memorable and uplifting!

CHAPTER SEVENTEEN

My Journey: Embracing Challenges, Finding Purpose

On 6th September 1971, I was born as the youngest of five children in Naduvakkad, Mampad Gram Panchayat. Right from my birth, my legs were completely disabled. Tragedy struck our poverty-stricken family when my father passed away just five months after my birth, leaving my hardworking mother to raise us with limited means. Despite our financial struggles, my siblings managed to attend school, while I could only watch them with teary eyes. My home, made of rolled mud walls and bamboo roof, felt even more isolated and disheartening. During the day, while my mother worked as a daily wage laborer, and my siblings attended school, I stayed at home accompanied by my elder aunt. My childhood lacked playful friends, but I had an unmatched interest in letters. Listening to stories and poems from my siblings became my routine.

One day, I started copying letters from my brother's textbook, and despite the challenges of holding a pen with my backward-folded fingers, I learned to write. My siblings helped me learn Malayalam, and I even started learning English and Hindi through guides gifted to me by kind individuals.

As I grew, I nurtured my love for reading, writing, and drawing. I wrote my first poem at eight and continued crafting stories and poems. Kunjunni Mash, a prominent writer, appreciated my work and encouraged me to write more. He became a guiding light in my literary journey. With determination and the support of my friends and family, I pursued my studies, passing the tenth-grade exam despite health challenges. I then became a Prerak for the Literacy Mission, working to promote education in my community.

In 2001, I married Safiya, who understood and supported my dreams. We have two children, Jouhar Jinan and Linsa Parvin. My aspiration to pursue a degree came true in 2014 when I enrolled in B.A. Malayalam through distance education. With hard work and support from well-wishers, I completed my undergraduate degree. I continue to study for my M.A. examination and pursue a diploma in psychology. My passion for reading, writing, and working for the welfare of the marginalized, especially differently abled individuals, remains strong. I envision a recreation center for differently abled individuals in Mampad, where they can learn job-oriented skills and be self-sufficient. Currently, I am a member of various organizations and work towards the uplifting of the differently abled and the abled. I am involved in initiatives like the seed pen production unit under the Thana Charitable Trust, empowering differently abled individuals for a livelihood.

My journey has taught me that disabilities don't define a person's potential. Through determination, support, and love, one can overcome challenges and make a meaningful impact in the world. I aspire to continue inspiring and empowering others as I embrace my life's purpose with enthusiasm and hope.

CHAPTER EIGHTEEN

A JOURNEY OF LEARNING AND GRATITUDE

The inability to receive elementary education as a day scholar has always been a source of pain, fueling my desire for knowledge and learning. Regardless of the obstacles, I have never shied away from opportunities to educate myself. When I shared my dream of pursuing a degree in psychology with Sivankutty Master, he became a profound source of inspiration. Learning psychology had been a long-standing aspiration, as I believed in the importance of being a good listener in a fast-paced world where people often overlook the joys and sorrows of others. A compassionate listener can ease the burden of the speaker, leading to a calm and fulfilling life.

Dr. Yasir, a dear friend and the organizer of Face Foundation, further encouraged me to pursue psychology, assuring me that it could transform my life. He connected me with Shafi Kalathingal, who welcomed my interest in psychology and guided me through the enrollment process for the 1-year Diploma in Psychology program at

Ryan Academy, Kondotty. Despite the challenges posed by Covid lockdowns, the classes conducted digitally on Saturdays from 2 PM to 4 PM were remarkably enriching. Shafi Sir's teaching style and interactive sessions added vibrancy to the learning experience. The chapters of psychology not only broadened my knowledge but also helped me evolve as a human being. During the internship period that followed in September, I had the privilege of interning at Malabar Medical Centre in Kondotty, where I counseled patients and prepared their case histories. This invaluable experience, however, highlighted the lack of facilities for differently abled individuals at public places like railway and bus stations. Accessible buildings with parking facilities for three-wheeled scooters and wheelchairs are essential for fostering inclusivity and ease for all individuals.

The last class of the internship at Ryan Academy in the Kondotty Bus Station Building was an unforgettable experience, where I was humbled by the support and kindness of my fellow classmates and faculty. Despite our diverse backgrounds and ages, we shared a unique bond of learning and friendship. Shafi Sir's thoughtful gesture during the class demonstrated his divine presence, not just as a teacher but as a compassionate soul. I am forever grateful to Almighty for surrounding me with such wonderful individuals, especially my wife Safiya and my children Jouhar Jinan and Linsa Parvin, whose support has been unwavering. I also offer my heartfelt prayers for the wellness and success of Ryan Academy and its caretaker, Shafi Sir.

As I step forward on this journey of learning and gratitude, I remain determined to contribute positively to the lives of others and continue growing as a compassionate and empathetic human being.

CHAPTER NINETEEN

P. S. Abdurahimankka - An Unforgettable Soul

Nearly two decades ago, I had the pleasure of meeting P. S. Abdurahimankka, a man with an everlasting smile and an ardent passion for reading. Introduced by IUML Naduvakkad Unit leader Maliyekkal Siddique, our meeting sparked a beautiful friendship. As we conversed, I realized that he was no ordinary person - his knowledge and wisdom were profound, making our discussions truly enriching.

In 2003, I rented a shop near the Thazhathangadi Madrasa of Mampad College Road, running a small cosmetic business. Abdurahimankka became a frequent visitor, and our talks evolved into deeper conversations. It was he who suggested that I keep registration forms in the shop due to my neat handwriting. He believed it would benefit those visiting the Panchayat Office and generate some income for me. Inspired by his idea, I started thinking about establishing a general service center, with Abdurahimankka providing not only the necessary forms and stamps but also guidance on their completion. This endeavor allowed me to assist many members of the public, particularly the marginalized and vulnerable. Abdurahimankka's story resonated deeply with the people of Mampad. Coming from Thrissur to work as a cigar laborer at the Chandraraj Beedi Company, he quickly became an integral part of the town's cultural and artistic community. He married from Pongallur and settled at Nalucent Colony, Pallikkunnu.

At the time, Pallikkunnu Colony faced severe poverty and destitution, a situation that prompted Abdurahimankka's social activism. He organized the colony inhabitants and spearheaded initiatives to improve their living conditions. Thanks to his relentless efforts, government funds flowed in, leading to the construction of houses, toilets, public wells, roads, and electrical connectivity. All the pocket roads were transformed into concrete ones, and an anganwadi and cultural center were established nearby. Abdurahimankka's dedication to these developments was unmatched.

Passionate about youth development, he was an active organizer of the Mampad Youths Arts and Sports Club and held positions at S.T.U at district and state levels. His dream of a new library building for Mampad was fueled by his love for reading and his desire to spread knowledge among the common taxpayers and students.

Abdurahimankka played a pivotal role in my own literary journey, introducing me to renowned books like "Freedom At Midnight," "The Bells are Ringing in

Haridwar," "Manju," "Kaalam," "The Diary of Anne Frank," "Ramayana Stories," and "1001 Nights." Our literary discussions at my shop, with the participation of Dr. Sivankutty, Babu Valiyaparamb, and others, led to the establishment of the Shalabam Literary Club at Mampad. Abdurahimankka and Paul Valayil served as guardians, I presided over the club, Sivankutty Master was the secretary, and Babu acted as the treasurer.

Even after undergoing a bypass surgery, Abdurahimankka continued to tirelessly work for public welfare, dressed in his white mundu and shirt, and always spreading smiles. His dedication to building a new library remained until his passing on Monday, 21 June 2021. P. S. Abdurahimankka's legacy will forever be remembered with admiration and gratitude. His contributions to society and his love for knowledge have left an indelible mark on our hearts. May the soul rest in peace. Heartfelt condolences to the dear ones.

CHAPTER TWENTY

A Day of Dreams and Discovery

Many of us dream when we travel, as we encounter sights that captivate our senses and ignite our imaginations. This truth holds even more profoundly for the differently abled, who often find themselves confined within the four walls of their homes, unable to fathom a world beyond.

It was in this context that the National Service Scheme volunteers of MES Mampad College conceived a plan to orchestrate an exclusive journey for the differently abled community in collaboration with the Mampad Palliative Centre. The date was etched in golden letters in our minds - March 11, 2023. On that remarkable day, MES Mampad College's reputation soared to new heights. We embarked on a journey with 40 physically and mentally challenged individuals, destined for Calicut, where the boundless waves of hope awaited us.

The efforts of the Palliative Centre officials, along with dedicated teachers such as Anas Sir, Rajesh Sir, Shameera Mam, and the enthusiastic participation of students like

Ashna, Sana, Niha, Sreenandha, Asif, Jilva, Nihal, Nidha, Faiz, Hiba, Najil, Rinha, Nizam, Sanan, Lashin, Haseeb, Anas, Amritha, and Fayad transformed this trip into an unforgettable memory.

The day commenced with the arrival of nurses from the palliative center and members of the 'Chuvadukal' Differently Abled Community on the college premises at 8 AM. The sight of NSS volunteers, who had prepared to lend their helping hands, added to our joy. The bus arrived shortly after half-past eight, and excitement filled the air as everyone eagerly boarded. The volunteers observed each person's expressions and offered assistance accordingly. A van, equipped with 20 wheelchairs, led the way, and our bus followed in tow. Our journey was a tapestry of merriment and delight. Inside the bus, the program began with a mesmerizing song by the talented differently abled individual, Majeedka.

The interaction with the volunteers made us momentarily forget our challenges, fostering a sense of belonging and camaraderie. The NSS volunteers left no stone unturned to ensure this trip would be etched in our memories. Their beautiful songs and joyful dances lifted our spirits, making us feel cherished. We mustn't overlook the invaluable role played by the palliative workers throughout the excursion. Witnessing students cum NSS volunteers wholeheartedly assisting every differently abled person, even in their most basic needs, left me speechless. Their compassion and dedication, despite having received only a one-day workshop on interacting with the differently abled, serve as a beacon of change.

Amidst our journey, our first stop was Beypore Harbour. We marveled at the sights and took a ferry ride, an experience that left an indelible mark on each one of us. The ferry, teeming with people and vehicles, transported us to a realm that felt like the heart of the ocean. Our happiness knew no bounds, evident in our radiant faces as we enjoyed breakfast by the water. Our next destination was the planetarium in Calicut, an entirely new experience for me. Inside, we ventured into an unfamiliar world, gazing at simulated planets, stars, comets, and celestial bodies. At that moment, all of us were enveloped in sheer happiness, relishing this unique chapter in our lives. Lunch was served in the open outside the planetarium, after which we headed to Kappad Beach. Thanks to wheelchair-friendly promenades, we were able to reach the shoreline and dip our feet into the saline water.

It was there that the NSS volunteers organized cultural programs that left us spellbound. Shada, a dedicated NSS volunteer, masterfully anchored the program. Ayshamall, Majeedka, and Shabana Asmi represented us, showcasing their talents in a beautiful display. In a heartwarming surprise, the volunteers presented us with a cake to celebrate the first anniversary of our society, the Chuvadukal Society. This coincidence added an unexpected and joyful touch to our day, drawing the attention of others who had come to visit the beach.

As the sun began its descent into the sea, college students continued to run tirelessly around us, relishing their roles as helpers. The powerful waves at twilight beckoned us further into the vastness of the sea. Many of us were witnessing the ocean for the first time, and we reveled in the sunset's beauty. At Kappad, where Vasco Da Gama first set foot in India to establish trade, my legs, and those of many others, touched saline water for the very first time. The daylight gave way to darkness after a day filled with satisfaction, joy, happiness, and contentment.

CHAPTER TWENTY-ONE

A Lovely Consideration

The degree of disability a person experiences is often a reflection of the consideration they receive, whether it be from their family or society at large. For those who find themselves dependent on others even for their most basic needs, this dependence can feel like a form of slavery. Yes, dependency is a form of servitude. However, when differently abled individuals depend on others who interact with them with kindness and compassion, this dependency no longer feels like enslavement. It becomes a shared understanding, where both the helper and the helped communicate effectively to provide the necessary assistance. In this context, such dependency ceases to be a form of bondage; instead, it becomes a meaningful exchange that paints a colorful rainbow in the minds of the differently abled.

It was precisely this feeling that accompanied us when the NSS volunteers of MES Mampad College took us on a joyful journey to Calicut. It was a unique experience for us, coming from an institution of this kind. Dr. Rajesh Monji, a renowned writer, teacher, and staff editor of MES

Mampad College, had shared with us his vision for the 2021-22 edition of the college magazine. He expressed the desire that it should resonate with the experiences of the differently abled and reflect their life stories. This initiative deeply moved me because society has often portrayed physically abled individuals as 'able' and those with physical challenges as 'disabled.' These individuals shattered that stereotype and courageously decided to embrace this theme. From that moment on, I felt a part of this journey, culminating in the publication of our magazine, 'Aakasham Thodunnavar' (Those Who Touch the Sky).

The cover design of our magazine proudly showcases 30 beautiful, smiling faces of our differently abled community members. Each page within contains stories of our resilience, dedication, struggles, and our unwavering determination to overcome adversity. The college's principal and the chief editor of the magazine, Dr. PP Manzur Ali, along with other editorial members, such as Dr. Sreeja, Dr. Sajid A Latheef, and Dr. Fausath Ali PP, inspired us to believe that we too matter to society. For differently abled individuals, this kind of encouragement is vital to help them navigate their paths forward.

The magazine's launch event was a vibrant affair, held in the vicinity of the Mampad Palliative Centre, adjacent to the shed that serves as the gathering place for 'Chuvadukal' community members. This is where we come together each month, sharing joy and laughter. At the event, every differently abled member proudly raised their magazine in their hands, a powerful and heartwarming sight. NSS volunteers played a crucial role in making this event a resounding success. Our community members sang songs and danced with infectious joy. Dr. Rajesh Sir graced us with a traditional song, leaving the audience deeply moved. The volunteers even trained the differently abled in crafting and simple magic tricks. Lunch for the day was generously sponsored by the NSS unit, leaving both our hearts and stomachs full. The volunteers promised to return with more engaging activities.

This experience taught us a valuable lesson: when differently abled individuals feel acknowledged and considered, their sense of disability gradually diminishes. As differently abled people navigate their lives, they may only be reminded of their disabilities when their journey pauses at a staircase without ramps or elevators. Therefore, regardless of the nature of the disability, we can all strive to follow the MES Mampad College model of inclusion, where differently abled members are cherished and treated with compassion. If educational institutions and society as a whole embrace this approach, differently abled individuals can perform remarkable feats in their lives, truly creating magic.

CHAPTER TWENTY-TWO

A Vision Unveiled - The Vocational Village

In the fabric of society, there exists a segment often overshadowed, suffering silently in the shadow of adversity - the Middle Class. While much attention is rightfully given to those with disabilities, the Middle Class, too, grapples with their own trials and tribulations. A compassionate society should extend its helping hand to those families struggling to put food on their table, regardless of party affiliations, gender, caste, or religion. Within the Middle Class, there lies a group of individuals enduring dire circumstances. These are people who might have once enjoyed prosperity, possibly inheriting wealth or engaging in successful business ventures. Yet, at some point in their journey through life, they have experienced the harsh blows of fate, losing their wealth and livelihoods, and finding themselves locked in a relentless struggle against hunger.

The Middle Class encompasses those who yearn for a place to call home, burdened with heavy bank loans, or facing the exorbitant costs of treating life-threatening illnesses. It includes widows, orphans, unmarried women, and many more who, above all, deserve empathy rather than mere sympathy. Empathy, the profound understanding that another's need is our own, fuels our determination to seek solutions for these societal issues. It is the belief that our assistance is not charity but the acknowledgment of their inherent rights. This profound empathy is the driving force behind my dream project - 'A Vocational Village.'

As a humble government employee stationed at the Pandikkad Rest House in the Public Works Department of the Government of Kerala, my responsibilities extend beyond my family's well-being. My vision was initially inspired by a desire to improve the quality of life for the differently-abled individuals who, confined to their rooms, yearned for opportunities beyond their physical limitations. Thus, I founded the 'Chuvadukal' differently-abled community, uniting members from various corners of Mampad. Through collaborative efforts with the Mampad Palliative Centre, we established a center where we conduct three daycares each month. These daycares encompass literacy classes, counseling sessions, motivation workshops, skill development programs, and cultural events. My heart swells with gratitude for the impact of these programs, which have not only supported the differently-abled but have also expanded to embrace the struggling Middle Class.

I initiated an umbrella-making workshop for them, and as my dream of a Vocational Village takes shape, I aspire to offer a thousand employment opportunities to those in need. In the face of skepticism from those who question how a seemingly insurmountable project could be undertaken, I offer a simple response, "A healthy mind is more vital than a healthy body." With this unwavering belief, I am confident in my ability to turn this dream into reality. Recent times have witnessed the realization of this vision as I took concrete steps to provide employment to those in need. We have trained individuals in the art of crafting umbrellas, producing pickles, crafting paper pens, seed pens, soaps, detergents, washing liquids, floor cleaning agents, and phenyl. As of September 2023, we have established twenty-two units operating at full capacity, with each unit comprising 10-15 members.

The majority are involved in umbrella and pickle production, which follows a simple yet effective process. For instance, consider a pickle-making unit, where arrangements are made with vegetable sellers for the necessary raw materials. Upon completion, the finished product is returned, and the pickle maker is compensated per packet produced. Registration for these units is facilitated through Kudumbasree Units at the Panchayat level, streamlining the process for marginalized individuals. Once established, all responsibilities are delegated to the unit level, with my commitment to provide necessary support when concerns or challenges arise. These small-scale initiatives foster self-sufficiency and independence among those involved. Moreover, they enable access to healthier, additive-free food options, benefitting both consumers and suppliers.

The implementation of other items mentioned in a similar fashion ensures that every marginalized individual has the opportunity to transform into the promise of a brighter tomorrow. In the heart of this endeavor lies the belief that by empowering the Middle Class and other marginalized groups with meaningful employment and dignified opportunities, we can sew the seeds of transformation and hope in the rich tapestry of our society. The Vocational Village stands as a testament to our unwavering commitment to building a more inclusive and empathetic world.

www.ingramcontent.com/pod-product-compliance
Lightning Source LLC
LaVergne TN
LVHW021201160826
845679LV00024B/2193

* 9 7 9 8 8 9 1 3 3 6 5 5 1 *